DAY DEVOTIONAL
31

her walk

THE JOURNEY WITHIN

God Bless,

Casey

CATRINA TILLMAN

DAY DEVOTIONAL 31

her walk
THE JOURNEY WITHIN

TRM
Publications

a division of TRM Enterprise, LLC

Copyright © 2017 Catrina Tillman
Published by TRM Publications
Post Office Box 16124
Atlanta, Georgia 30321
www.trm-enterprises.com

TRM Publications is a division of
TRM Enterprises, LLC, Atlanta, Georgia

Printed in the United States of America

Cover Design by Gifted Dezyns Graphics & Printing

www.gifteddezyns.com

ISBN 9780692975084

Stay connected with Catrina Tillman

 @ She_ministries

www.sheministries.net

Email: S.H.EMinistries@icloud.com

It gives me great joy to offer commendations to Catrina Tillman as she shares her journey with the world. God has continued to use this vessel of a woman for the upbuilding of His Kingdom.

This life-changing devotional promises to be the key that unlocks the roadblocks that have kept you stagnant. Receive your blessing and move forward on your journey.

Cynthia P. Smith
Woman's Auxiliary President
National Baptist Convention, USA, INC.

Her Walk Special Thanks

To my best friend, my love, my husband, Ezra Tillman Jr, thank you for your unconditional love and support. You saw the author in me before I knew she existed. Thank you for pushing me into my destiny and praying me through this process. My walk is smoother with you beside me. I love you!

To my 4 Heartbeats; Ezra III, Micah, Isaac, and Baby Luke, thank you for being patient with mommy during the process of writing this book. You are my reason, drive, and motivation. My journey is filled with purpose because of you. To Marcus and Ashleigh thank you for supporting me and sharing my excitement.

To my sister circle, thank you for your prayers, support, and accountability during this entire writing process. The late night calls, and early morning prayers kept me focused. Our bond is real and our sisterhood is authentic...Love each of you dearly!

To God be the Glory!

Contents

Introduction

She is the daughter, sister, friend, wife, mother, co-worker, she is the boss. She cooks, cleans, organizes, and multitasks. She loves, cries, hurts, and laughs. She-Her-You-Me…We are every woman! We wear many hats, and too often the gravity of them can become overwhelming. Trying to conquer this thing called balance, while searching for identity and purpose is a task within itself.

Being the wife of a Pastor and a mother of 4 boys, I often find myself in the midst of being everything to everyone. But God! His Holy word helps me every time I feel like I'm "losing" me. Whether it's reading one scripture or a whole book, I am sure to discover myself in His word. God's word establishes us; it brings about identity and purpose.

Some say that life is the best teacher. I disagree; I say the Bible is the best teacher. However, through life's experiences, there have been times when I've felt alone, vulnerable, afraid, not worthy, weak, unloved...
the list goes on and on. I'm certain as women we all can identify with some of these feelings if not all. No matter what you're going through God's word has an answer.

With each day new challenges arrive. It is my prayer that these 31-day devotionals meet you where you are. Some are practical while others are "out the box", but all of these devotionals are infused with the word of God, inspired by everyday life situations, feelings, and the paths that we travel.

Enjoy!

Day 1

T.A.G. You're IT!

" $\mathscr{B}$ ut when you pray, go into your room, close the door and pray to your Father, who is unseen. Then your Father, who sees what is done in secret, will reward you" (Matthew 6:6) NIV

Remember being a child and playing tag with your friends? In a time of pure boredom, tag was the go to game of choice. No matter how many children there were, everyone could participate and play. We would run around until we were tired chasing after each other, out of breath and thirsty, which eventually caused the game to come to an end.

What if as adults, we carried that childhood playing mentality over into our adult/spiritual life. What if we chased God until we became tired? Running after His will, His truth, His word, until we became exhausted? What if we searched for God as if we were playing "Hide and Seek"?

Being a mom of four boys, I get it. As women, we don't always have time to do an in depth study of God's word. The duties of life are forever calling, with a great expectation for us to answer and produce results with excellence. It may not be motherhood for you, but perhaps you have a demanding career, an elderly parent, or involvement in different organizations that require much of your attention. Whatever "it" is, there is and will always be something that is demanding your time. But I was once told, you find time for what's important to you.

Application

Transparent moment; there have been times where I've put the needs and demands of my children, and husband before my relationship with God. Constantly pouring so much of myself into others, only to find myself depleted and empty at days end. Something had to give, something had to change! It was time for me to make time for what was and "is" important.

Time Alone with God (T.A.G) it`s a necessity! Spending time with Him and in His presence brings about a balance and a state of peace that is unexplainable. For it is Him that created us, which means He understands how we think, how we are wired, what stresses us out, and what desires we have. When no one else understands you or what you're going through, that's the time for you to tap yourself and say "T.A.G Your It."

Go into your secret closet, be it in the car while driving with no music on, your prayer room, the bathroom...wherever! The point is that you get to that quiet place with no distractions where it's just you and God. Lay it all before Him. It could even be that scheduled time that you set aside daily to read the Bible. Make your relationship and commitment to God a priority and watch His promises for your life unfold!

My T.A.G. this month is doing the following...

_____

_____

_____

_____

_____

_____

_____

_____

_____

_____

_____

T.A.G. You're It!

_____

_____

_____

_____

_____

_____

_____

_____

_____

_____

_____

_____

_____

_____

_____

_____

_____

_____

_____

_____

_____

_____

_____

_____

_____

_____

_____

_____

_____

Her Walk Day 1

FOCUS

" Commit to the Lord whatever you do, and he will establish your plans" (Proverbs 16:3) NIV

If I could request one thing from God that I think we all could benefit from, it would be to add more time to our day. It seems like no matter how well you plan, there's just not enough time in a day to complete our task.

As women, we can be very ambitious and driven when it comes to our career and personal goals. But sometimes the demands that come with the titles may cause us to get off our path. After you've spent the day being everything to everyone on the job, at home, and in your social life, where does one find time to develop an idea or a plan?

Transparent moment; just writing this book alone has been challenging for me. Being the wife of a Pastor, a mother of 4 boys (our youngest being a newborn), and the guardian of my niece and nephew; finding quiet time to hear from God, execute my thoughts, and actually type a complete sentence, has been extremely challenging. However, when you know that God has given you the vision and desire, you find the time to block out distractions and focus! It's much easier said than done, but the fact is, with God it CAN be done!

Application

Have you noticed in a horse race, they wear blinders? The purpose is to keep the horse focused from being distracted, which could cause them to ultimately lose the race. Just like in our lives, we must place imaginary blinders to block out distractions that keep us from winning! Remember, you are guaranteed to win with Christ! If it's writing a book, starting your own business, going back to school, or developing new technology, place Jesus at the core to stay focused.

We must not lose sight of the fact that we need Christ in ALL that we do! Our personal plans, goals, and desires are nothing without God. Psalm 37:4 (NIV) says "Take delight in the Lord, and he will give you the desires of your heart." Pray over your goals and dreams and always incorporate Christ in your plans, and watch the path to success unfold.

Today I will focus on _____

_____

_____

_____

_____

_____

By blocking out_____

_____

_____

_____

_____

_____

_____

_____

_____

_____

_____

Focus

_____
_____
_____
_____
_____
_____
_____
_____
_____
_____
_____
_____
_____
_____
_____
_____
_____
_____
_____
_____
_____
_____
_____
_____
_____
_____

J.U.M.P.

"In God I trust and am not afraid. What can man do to me?" (Psalm 56:11) NIV

Isn't it amazing how at times, we give energy to the wrong things? Let's just be honest, there are times we've allowed doubt, insecurities, and even fear to steal our dreams like a thief in the night. The doubt of not believing that your vision will be actualized, the insecurity of not having the support from others, and the fear of not being successful can cause one to freeze right where they stand, lacking the will to be self-determined and motivated. In return, the focus shifts into discovering new reasons why you should not take the action needed to J.U.M.P!

That's right where I found myself. Stuck in the daily routine called LIFE! My routine consist of waking up, getting the boys ready for school, making breakfast, making lunch, giving them their vitamins, sending them out the door, washing clothes, folding clothes, putting clothes up (ugh… I hate folding clothes), running errands, getting boys off the bus, cooking dinner, going over homework, sending them to bed, talking to my husband about his day, making him watch one of my favorite chick flicks…and finally off to bed. Only to start the cycle all over again.

But what about my goals and dreams, what happened to the excitement of life. I found myself lost in the lives of others, only to lose sight of the purpose and vision God had given me for my life. It was at this point I finally understood the meaning of being alive but not living. I knew in order for me to get back in tuned with myself, I had to do one thing,…J.U.M.P

Whether it's jumping towards something, into something, over something (or someone), we must first abide by the necessary steps to be successful in landing on our mark. Are you ready to J.U.M.P?

Application

J- Join forces with like-minded people

The old saying is "Birds of a feather flock together". I find this to be true. Who you surround yourself with speaks volume of who you are. Building your own personal network of people is vital when preparing to jump. Having a mentor that can guide you and give you wise counsel, or having an accountability partner that will keep you focused and on track, will aid you in being successful. Build you a network of support! Proverbs 15:22 (NIV) "Plans fail for lack of counsel, but with many advisers they succeed."

U- Understand it's a process

Anything worth having is worth working for. Success doesn't come over night. Think about the process of establishing a relationship. Getting to know a person for who they really are and not their representative, takes time. You have to go through ups and downs to get the full picture of who they are, and how they respond in certain situations. So whether it's trusting your heart and jumping into love, or writing that book you always said you would write, trust the process! In due time the dream will be actualized. Habakkuk 2:3 (NIV) "For the revelation awaits an appointed time; it speaks of the end and will not prove false. Though it linger, wait for it; it will certainly come and will not delay."

M- Make it Happen!

Dreams without action is nothing but sleep. A jump is never completed without taking action first. The movement, the work, the discipline must all come from you. God has given you the idea, the vision, the dream and it will come true. Don't let it die on your watch. JUMP! James 2:26 (NKJV) "...faith without works is dead..."

P-Pray

Often we begin praying for the desires of our hearts, but when God answers our prayers, our line of communication with Him concerning that matter slowly comes to a halt. My mother always told me, you have to pray your way through the test and pray your way to the victory. You will find that throughout this action of jumping, the act of prayer must travel with you. Even after you land on your personal mark of success, continue to be prayerful that your next landing mark can and will be actualized.

1 Thessalonians 5:17 "Pray without ceasing" (NKJV)

I'm going to J.U.M.P. by doing...

_____

_____

_____

_____

_____

_____

_____

Day 4

Mask Off

❧

"Search me, God, and know my heart; test me and know my anxious thoughts. See if there is any offensive way in me, and lead me in the way everlasting" (Psalm 139:23-24) NIV

Question: When was the last time you looked in the mirror? Beyond the hair, clothes, and make-up. Oh, I know, it's uncomfortable. There are some things in the mirror that stare back at you that you're not happy about. Things that you wish you could get rid of. Things we are ashamed of, things that we can't let go of. Guilt, bitterness, jealousy, unforgiveness, envy, brokenness; they all stare right back at you.

Some of us have carried these feelings and emotions for years. So much so that they have become our identity. We walk around wearing the "I'm ok" mask all day long, only to be fragmented pieces of a woman who was once whole. Fearful of others coming in contact with our true self, we allow people to meet and interact with our representative. Yet God tells us in Isaiah 41:13 (NIV) "...Do not fear; I will help you." However, this kind of help comes by way of being honest and vulnerable to God.

The truth is all of us have done something that is displeasing to God. Romans 3:23 (NIV) tells us that "for all have sinned and fall short of the glory of God". Yet there's something about releasing your strongholds, flaws, and shortcomings to God. There's freedom in unmasking that which has held you in bondage.

Application

God is concerned about your well-being and growth in Him. Although He is the creator of life and He is omniscient, we must still invite Him in to cleanse us and make us whole. In order for Him to identify us as His own creation, we must remove the mask to be recognized. Then and only then, can we allow God to make us whole.

Let's free ourselves today! Let today be the day that you come from behind that mask. Expose your true self in the presence of God and receive a make-over. One that is made new and whole and full of identity and purpose.

Reflect

_____

_____

_____

_____

_____

_____

_____

_____

_____

_____

_____

_____

_____

_____

_____

_____

Her Walk Day 4

Day 5

Are You Dressed Yet?

"*She* is clothed with strength and dignity; she can laugh at the days to come" (Proverbs 31:25) NIV

We all have that one girlfriend who takes forever to get dress. The date has been scheduled for over a month, you give her a reminder call the week of, not to mention you've discussed your attire for the event. Despite all the reminders and prep talk, she still is perplexed on what fashion statement she will make the hour before you both are planning to be in attendance.

Transparent moment; there are times that the girlfriend I'm describing is me! So I can totally relate, LOL. And I get it, being a woman requires preparations and maintenance. Hair, nails, makeup, clothing, and shoes (did I say shoes); they all play into the message that you want to convey to the world. Your appearance speaks for you before you can speak for yourself. However, there are times that we get so engulfed in things and not substance that our message can get misconstrued with our mission.

Application

As a follower of Christ, we should not only represent His goodness and grace by way of our outer appearance, but we should also make sure that our inner attitude is just as attractive. The garments of both strength and honor are created and developed from within, yet they are seen from the outside.

The garment of strength represents the firmness of mindset that is displayed in the storms of life. Having not been shaken, distressed, or moved by the winds that may blow. It means you are rooted and secure in who you are and most importantly, whose you are!

Are You Dressed Yet?

The garment of honor speaks to respect and integrity that is worn by a child of God. Not only is it given, but it is also received. There's a certain level of dignity that is carried by a child of God. Knowing that you represent the King in all that you do, the honor that comes along in wearing that crown is reverenced daily.

Your shine should not only come from the sequence, glitter, and bling that are perfectly placed on your clothing, wrist, or fingers. It should be dimmed compared to the light that comes from within. What you wear on the outside should only be a prelude of what's within. Many will compliment you on what you wear, but as we know, it's not what you wear, it's how you wear it! No matter what today or tomorrow brings, make sure you are dressed appropriately to endure what comes your way.

I can apply this devotional to my life by...

Are You Dressed Yet?

_____

_____

_____

_____

_____

_____

_____

_____

_____

_____

_____

_____

_____

_____

_____

_____

_____

_____

_____

_____

_____

_____

_____

_____

Day 6
REWIND

"*F*orget the former things; do not dwell on the past. See, I am doing a new thing!…" (Isaiah 43:18-19a) NIV

What's your favorite movie? You know the one you watch over and over. The one that none of your family members like watching with you because you know every word from beginning to end. Yes, that one! Movies are an amazing form of art. They are created to tell a story while connecting with our emotions. In a sense, we can view our own individual lives as a movie.

Just as a movie is created for a large audience to view, your life is on the big screen. People are viewing your life right from the front row, while others are in the back. They all see the same screen at the same time. Some cheer during your scenes of perseverance, some cry at your moments of sadness, while others sit back eating popcorn taking mental notes of your failures.

I find it ironic, that right at the moment you decide to change your life, reposition yourself, and live for Jesus, the past comes to visit. The timing is almost exact; your mind is made up and then...BOOM! The ex-boyfriend appears out of the blue, your girlfriend wants to relive your college days, or the family member that wants to remind you of your past.

What happens when it's not the ex, the girlfriend, or the family member, but it's YOU pressing the rewind button in your life?

Application

We hold onto thoughts, events, and people of our past that God has already delivered, forgiven and freed us from. Yet we find just enough space to feature them in a reoccurring role in our lifetime movie.

Those things that are of old, let them be just that…OLD. Sometimes you have to let your past die so that YOU can live. Let it go, release it. You now have access to the newness of life and all the abundance that comes with it by way of your obedience and faithfulness. Luke 9:62 (NKJV) says, "But Jesus said to him, 'No one, having put his hand to the plow, and looking back, is fit for the kingdom of God'." The only time we should press rewind is to look back as a point of reference to see just how far God has brought us!

My Top 3 things I need to let go of are?

1._____

_____

_____

_____

2._____

_____

_____

_____

_____

3._____

_____

_____

_____

_____

Day 7
Less is More

" *H*e must become greater; I must become less..." (John 3:30) NIV

Transparent moment; I get in my own way, more than anything else. Yes, it's true. I'm sure we all can attest to this statement. There are times I complicate situations simply by over thinking or trying to force the results. I've allowed insecurities and self-doubt to get the best of me, and there are plenty of times I simply give up. In each occurrence, I realized that my trust was misplaced and that I was depending more on my willpower oppose to aligning with the will of God. This is a recipe for failure.

In order for growth to take place, submission to God's will is essential. We must move out of our own way in order for Christ to lead us the right way. Now granted, this sounds simple and even cliché, but it's true. It's easier said than done and truth be told, this is a major struggle in our spiritual growth.

The one person you know better than anyone is yourself! The good, the bad, and the ugly. You know you! That makes it easy for you to trust your own voice, depend on yourself, to get things done, and to make it happen. It's easy for you to rely on your own instincts when you are in tune with self. However, all of this self-empowerment can cause more havoc than help. The moment that you allow your voice to overshadow the voice of God, is the moment that you begin to be your own god. FACT!

Application

"Then He said to them all: "Whoever wants to be my disciple must deny themselves and take up their cross daily and follow me."(Luke 9:23)NIV.
In order for us to gain more in Christ, we must be willing

to lose ourselves in the process. Our flesh is too attracted to the sinful ways of this world. Therefore we must die to self so that we may live in Christ! The process of denying self is a daily shedding of our flesh. Getting rid of our ways, our attitude, and our insecurities, just to name a few. There is so much for us to gain in Christ. His protection, His blessings, and His will for our life. When we place our agenda before His, we risk losing it all.

On this day let your prayer be simple. Lord less of me and more of you!

I need to be more like Christ by getting rid of ...
1._____

_____

_____

_____

2._____

_____

_____

_____

3._____

_____

_____

_____

Her Walk Day 7

Day 8
Shine Bright

"*In* the same way, let your light shine before others, that they may see your good deeds and glorify your Father in heaven" (Matthew 5:16) NIV

I can remember attending Sunday school as a young child learning and singing the song, "This little light of mine…" At the time, I thought it was just a catchy song, not fully understanding the meaning of "the light." It wasn't until I became an adult with some life experiences under my belt that I came to the knowledge and understanding of "this little light of mine."

Light has a way of changing the atmosphere. One of the first things I do after waking up, is open all the curtains and blinds. I call this process waking up the house, LOL. This helps jumpstart my day be it a sunny or foggy morning. Daylight helps bring life into the home.

Similar to our daily lives, the light that we carry as a follower of Christ, must shine bright for others to see. While the sins of this world continues to create darkness, we the "Called Out", according to 1 Peter 2:9 are chosen to shine bright. Despite the dark tactics of the enemy, we must not allow it to overshadow God's light within us.

Application

This "Little light of ours", has the power to attract. Like a moth to a flame, the light that we carry draws others to us. We must realize this light is a gift not only for yourself but to share with others as we journey closer to Christ. Being conscious of every step taken, action made, and word spoken; fully understanding that someone is always watching. While everyone can't fit your shoes, some can still walk your path! They may not read the Bible, but they will read YOU. They will study you to see if you are really who you say you are, if your lifestyle matches your walk, and if you treat people how you want to be treated. This is why we can't afford for our light to dim. The light that we have is not our own, it belongs to God.

Psalm 119:105 (NIV) says, "Your word is a lamp for my feet, a light on my path." This little light of ours is energized by the Word of God and focused on its destination in Christ Jesus, leading us and those that the Lord has placed in our paths to a place of peace, blessings, and growth.

I will let my light shine by doing the following...

_____

_____

_____

_____

_____

_____

_____

_____

_____

_____

_____

_____

_____

_____

_____

_____

_____

Shine Bright

Day 9
Our Secret Weapon

"With the tongue we praise our Lord and Father, and with it we curse human beings, who have been made in God's likeness" (James 3:9) NIV

No matter your race, background, or social status; we all have this one thing in common. It's our gift of tongue! Not in the spiritual sense but in the physical and carnal. Oh yes, give us the right situation, circumstance, or conversation that's not in our favor, and watch us tap into our secret weapon of tongues and tell you where you can go and how fast you can get there...LOL

It's a small part of our body but holds so much power! Proverbs 18:21 (NIV) states, "The tongue has the power of life and death, and those who love it will eat its fruit." Often times we can become very opinionated and stuck on what we believe to be true. However, I've learned timing plays a very critical part in determining if we start a war or bring peace to a situation by way of our tongue.

Transparent moment; when my husband and I have had a disagreement and I was "in my feelings" I felt the urge to say whatever came to mind to prove my point. Nevertheless, I was unsuccessful in getting the results I wanted; because my response was impromptu and my approach and timing, were not in sync. Therefore, I did not hear the heart of my husband, causing more tension between us, thanks to my tongue.

Application

Proverbs 15:1 (NIV) says, "A gentle answer turns away wrath, but a harsh word stirs up anger." Consulting God on when to speak and what to say can cause the conversation to work in your favor. When I have something really important to say, I always pray that God will guide my tongue, open the ears and heart of the person I'm speaking with. We must use our secret weapon wisely to give life to a dead situation and bring peace to a war. This is why prayer is so important!

There are moments when God will reveal that now is not the time or place to speak your heart. It may be uncomfortable to hold your tongue, especially when you KNOW your point of view is correct. There are times you have to lose the fight in order to win the battle.

As you go forth in your day today, keep in mind that you have control over your response and that God has control over the outcome!

Reflect

_____

_____

_____

_____

_____

_____

_____

_____

_____

_____

_____

_____

_____

Our Secret Weapon

Day 10

A Seat at the Table

" *You* prepare a table before me in the presence of my enemies…" (Psalm 23:5) NIV

We've all been around them, heard them, or even witness them in action. Some of us may have been victims of their tactics. It's as if they wake up in the morning with the sole intent to discourage, hurt, or even harm us. Yes, I'm talking about HATERS! You know that person at your job that's always trying to take credit for your hard work or that person who always has something negative to say. Yes, the haters! They are never truly happy for you, always wanting to compare your success to theirs, and are constantly trying to outshine you. But I was once told, only a dim light can be out shined! Catch it!

Being a child of God automatically subjects you to hater-ism. The Bible speaks of these individuals and calls them "workers of iniquity." Even Jesus had haters. The Sadducees and Pharisees were always present trying to deny who Jesus was, and the power and gifts that He embodied. This idea of speaking ill will and trying to set traps is nothing new. It's bound to happen.

However, I truly believe Romans 8:28 (NIV) when it says, "And we know that in all things God works for the good of those who love him, who have been called according to his purpose." Even your haters or those workers of iniquity that are present in your life, yes they too are part of God's plan. The question we have to ask ourselves is why this person is placed in our path, on our job, or in our family? What am I to learn and gain from their evildoings?

Life suggests that obstacles reveal who we really are, not achievements. As much as we run from drama, crisis, and trauma; the truth is we really don't know what we are made of until we have been tested. Have you ever noticed that after an achievement, soon to follow is a setback, trap, or attack? In your moment of celebration, achievements, and victories there's a wolf in sheep clothing waiting to serve you a taste of insecurity and uncertainty. That's your table!

See there's a difference between being in the room vs. sitting at the table! Those that are in the room may have been invited, but they are not a distinguished guest, they are not the V.I.Ps. No, those that are in the room, are there to talk amongst each other about those that are sitting at the table. Your table represents victory, and your seat represents comfort, and status.

So how do you get a seat at the table? Well, the first step is to make up in your mind that you're going to enter the room! In other words, realizing that you have what it takes to persevere, to push, and press your way through to meet your destiny. Because this room is full of your enemies! They are present to look you up and down, to tell you you're not good enough, to remind you of what you use to be, and how you don't deserve to have a seat! Are you willing to walk in a room full of snakes ready to take a bite?

Application

Once you decide that you have what it takes to enter the room…then it's all about claiming what's yours. The table is reserved under your name! That job that you're praying about has already been assigned to you. That husband that you're praying about, is already in route to find you! Whatever it is, be it big or small, if God has it reserved for you, IT'S YOURS!!! Isaiah 54:17 (NKJV) says it best; "no weapon formed against you shall prosper,..." No snake filled room, no worker of iniquity, no hater; can stop you from receiving what God has for you.

You've been through the valley of the shadow of death, you've experienced rock bottom, you've lost friends that you thought were in your corner, and you've lost some fights to win the battle! Now that time has come for you to take your seat. Your table of victory is set, now take your seat and allow your enemies to watch you eat!!!

Read Psalm 59:2 & 1 Peter 5:8-9 & Reflect

_____

_____

_____

_____

_____

_____

_____

_____

_____

_____

_____

_____

_____

_____

_____

_____

Day 11
Lady in Waiting

"But as for me, I watch in hope for the Lord, I wait for God my Savior; my God will hear me" (Micah 7:7) NIV

In a world that is driven off time, everything is fast paced. No one likes to wait for anything. The sooner I can get a product or service done, the better. Because who has time to waste, right? As women, our to-do list is always running over. As soon as we check something off, 3 to 5 things are added right back on. There's never enough time in a day, and the demands of life never stop.

The unfortunate part is that we have allowed societies demand on time to spill over into our spiritual life. We take that same frustration and mindset and turn that into "God hurry up and make this happen." But yet, we will say in the same breath, I trust God. Waiting is not an easy thing to do and exercising patience is a process within itself!

Ever been in a long line? Do you find that time goes by quicker if you read a book or check your email? See waiting on God to move and give you an answer doesn't give you permission to check out of your spiritual routine while you're waiting. The benefits that come from waiting is determined upon your consistency while waiting! Devotion, meditation, and prayer should remain in your daily routine during your waiting season. You will find that in this season of eagerness, your relationship with God will develop even more if you continue to seek Him.

Application

Waiting on God puts us in a very vulnerable state because we realize that the outcome or answer is out of our control. However, we must not allow our vulnerability to discourage us from maximizing all that God has in store for us during this time of development.

Continue to seek God and get all that you can during this time. James 1:4 (NKJV) says, "But let patience have its perfect work, that you may be perfect and complete, lacking nothing". The process of patience produces the benefit package of perfection. You will find that not only will time go by faster, but when you get your answer, you will be ready and prepared to accept the outcome.

During my waiting season, I plan to do the following...

_____

_____

_____

_____

_____

_____

_____

_____

_____

_____

_____

_____

_____

_____

_____

_____

_____

_____

_____

_____

_____

_____

_____

_____

_____

_____

_____

_____

_____

_____

_____

_____

_____

_____

_____

_____

_____

_____

_____

_____

_____

_____

_____

Day 12

Faith it until you Make it

" *N*ow faith is the substance of things hoped for, the evidence of things not seen" (Hebrews 11:1) NKJV

I don't know where I would be without my faith! It keeps me, it sustains me, and it reassures me that God is with me regardless of how things look. Life has its own little way of throwing us off track. It seems like just when things are going well, out of nowhere all hell breaks loose. Family members begin to act up, job responsibilities seem to pile up, not to mention the added stress has disguised itself in the form of 10 extra pounds.

Maybe you haven't experienced any of these, but I'm sure you can fill in the blank when you wanted to yell "ENOUGH". Well, one thing that I've come to learn is that yelling never fixed anything, and after you yell guess what, the problem is still there! So now what? It's at that pivotal moment, the moment when you face your problems, concerns, and issues square in the face and say, "I'm going to make it, I'm going to win, and I'm going to overcome! It's in that moment that you activate your faith!

See "faithing" it until you make it is not about tricking yourself into a falsehood just so you can get through the moment. No, it's placing the promises of God in the moment, so that you can get through. It's reminding yourself that God will supply all your needs (Philippians 4:19), that God is a healer (Jeremiah 30:17), and that God is with you at all time (Hebrews 13:5). It's believing that the impossible is possible. It's seeing yourself already on the side of victory when the battle has just begun!

Application

Faith brings substance to hope. Those things that you are wishing for and hoping to take place, faith provides the evidence of that which is to come. Outside of prayer, faith is another tool that can be used to secure success. When doors get closed in your face, when people tell you no you can't do it, faith pushes through and reminds you that "I can do ALL things through Christ who strengthens me" (Philippians 4:13) NIV.

Trusting God and His Word will give your faith longevity. The devil is always plotting on ways to tear at our faith and replace it with doubt. Faith and doubt are like oil and water, they just don't mix. We must feed our faith with God's word so that we have something firm to stand on other than our hopes and wishes.

Today, focus on providing nutrition to your faith by way of God's word.

Reflection

_____

_____

_____

_____

_____

_____

_____

_____

_____

_____

Faith it until you Make it

_____

_____

_____

_____

_____

_____

_____

_____

_____

_____

_____

_____

_____

_____

_____

_____

_____

_____

_____

_____

_____

_____

_____

_____

_____

Day 13
Who's the Boss?

"And whatever you do, do it heartily, as to the Lord and not to men…" (Colossians 3:23) NKJV

I can remember being a part of the workforce before I became a stay at home mom. I've had supervisors that I absolutely loved, and others I didn't click well with. Regardless of how I felt about them, my purpose of being there was to work. Granted, there were days I didn't feel like it, days I didn't want to be there, days I just didn't feel like being bothered. Yet and still the work had to be done!

One thing I've always been clear about are my job duties. These were very important for me to understand and know as an employee. The job duties simply speak to what is expected of you on a daily basis. Your success in a position is based on how well you accomplished those task. Your raise is based on how well and how often you performed your responsibilities. In other words, it's what determines your growth in the position and in the company. And it is taken into account when reviewed by your supervisor aka, the BOSS!

Now the boss is the person you want to please. You want to be on "good" terms with the boss. Confrontation, lack of communication, and continuous misunderstanding are all signs that you are not pleasing the boss! See, we must keep in mind that in most cases our boss has a boss that he/she must answer to. They are responsible for seeing that not only their job is completed, but your job as well.

Application

However, we must keep in the front of our mind as a child of God, who we really work for! Often times we get so caught up in pleasing people, even though they may be our boss, our parents, our husbands, our friends and so on, that we lose sight of pleasing God! Truth be told, man has no heaven or hell to place us in, God does. Therefore our focus should be on pleasing Him and not man.

Now don't get me wrong, your boss on your job is still your boss, LOL. And you should want to please them; however, it's something about carrying the Spirit of God with you wherever you go and in all that you do. Being a people pleaser will only alter your own identity conforming into what other people want you to be for their pleasure. But being a God pleaser will grant you unlimited benefits of blessings that will be for your pleasure. Once we change our lens on who we really work for, whether you work in Corporate America, you're an Entrepreneur, or a Domestic Engineer (aka...stay at home mom), let your works be pleasing in the sight of God first. For He has a benefit package that is eternal!

Read Luke 12:5 and reflect...

_____

_____

_____

_____

_____

_____

_____

_____

Who's the Boss?

_____

_____

_____

_____

_____

_____

_____

_____

_____

_____

_____

_____

_____

_____

_____

_____

_____

_____

_____

_____

_____

_____

_____

_____

Day 14

You Got Next!

" *A*nd let us not grow weary while doing good, for in due season we shall reap if we do not lose heart" (Galatians 6:9) NIV

Have you ever been in that space where you asked yourself, "When will my breakthrough come?" You see everyone around you doing good in life, living their dreams, traveling the world, dressing in fine clothing, eating at all the fine restaurants, etc. And yet, here you are with the same drive and ambition, however, you can't seem to catch a break. It can cause you to ask yourself, "what am I doing wrong?" You begin to question your own motives, doubt begins to creep in which causes you to devalue your gifts and talents. That feeling of discouragement has now matured to a feeling of defeat.

The truth is, everything we need to succeed, we already have. Each of us was born with different gifts and talents that were tailor made and designed for us as individuals. Your dreams are birthed out of the passion your gifts produce. You have what it takes to make your dreams a reality.

I can hear you saying, why hasn't this happened? It's a one-word answer...TIMING! See often times we get frustrated, discouraged, and stressed out because we expect things to happen in the time that we see fit.

Application

We never really take into consideration the importance of timing. Ecclesiastes 3:1 (NKJV) tells us "To everything there is a season, a time for every purpose under heaven." Which tells us and confirms the fact that you're right where you're supposed to be in the process. See, we think that it's our hard work that secures our success, but in essence, it's the timing that God allows doors to open in our favor that produces our success. Our job is to be fully prepared to walk through.

Everything that God creates has a purpose. That idea that you have, just didn't come out the clear blue sky. God placed it there for you to pursue it. He also equipped you with the tools that are needed to bring it to life. Your hard work and dedication thus far have brought you to this point. That gift that has been placed inside of you will come forth at its appointed time, but in the meantime between time, plan your work, and work your plan! The finish line is near!

"But you, be strong and do not let your hands be weak, for your work shall be rewarded." (2 Chronicles 15:7) NKJV

Reflect...

_____

_____

_____

_____

_____

_____

_____

_____

_____

_____

_____

Her Walk Day 14

Day 15
Lesson from my Stiletto's

 " *He* makes my feet like the feet of deer and sets me on my high places" (Psalm 18:33) NKJV

I can remember being a young girl running to my mother's room, going into her closet, and pulling out a pair of her high heels; placing them on my tiny feet, and trying to walk in them. Too often I would find myself on the ground, only feeling determined to get right back up and try it all over again.

Fast forward some years later, as an adult, I have grown a special bond with high heels. They are a form of art, a great accessory, and a conversation piece. Take a simple black dress and add the right pair of heels and it will transform that which was once simple into something spectacular!

Nevertheless, if we slide on our spiritual lens, we can learn a valuable lesson from one of God's greatest gifts to women... High Heels!

For some women, it's uncomfortable to walk in high heels. Anything over 4 inches is difficult for the average woman to walk in. As a Christian, that's just how our walk in Christ is, difficult, but rewarding. There are so many things around us that hinder us from walking a straight path. Road blocks here and there, cracks for us to fall into, and temptations to slow us down. There's always something! Just when you make your mind up to get your walk right with God, good ole' temptation comes knocking at the door. We must remind ourselves that God doesn't tempt us, He TESTS us (See James 1:13-15 & 1 Corinthians 10:13). Just like those high heels, life can be a test to walk in!

Every pair of stilettos has a sole and a heel. First, let's talk about the sole. The sole of the shoe is where most, if not all the pressure of the foot is placed. Now ladies, we know the higher the heel the more intense the pressure. However, shoe designers have heard our cry, and have anchored the sole with a platform to relieve some pressure. Just like our walk in God, our SOUL feels the pressure of the world, temptation, and sin! Our high heels teach us our SOUL must be anchored in Christ to make our walk more comfortable!

Oh but the heel, ahhhhh yes... the heel. This is my favorite part of the shoe. A shoe is a shoe, but once it graduates to its full maturity stage, it then becomes a pair of heels! The heel of the shoe is what sustains our balance. Not everyone can wear a pair of 4 ½ or 5-inch heels. These types of shoes are only reserved for the risk takers. We've all seen those who attempt to strut, but the walk just doesn't quite flow correctly. It's because their balance is off.

Application

Our heels teach us that in our daily walk, we must have balance in our lives. As women, we juggle so many things at once, but balance is essential for us to maintain peace of mind. At the very core of our lives and all that comes with it, the Word of God and a relationship with Jesus gives us the balance we need to endure this rocky path called life! Just as our high heels allow us to step high, the word of God elevates our mind, spirit, and soul!

So the next time you grab those pair of heels out your closet, look at them with a smile of appreciation that they deserve for the lessons they have taught us. Let's be "Risk Takers" and Step High!

Lesson from my Stiletto's

I can apply this devotional in the following ways...

_____

_____

_____

_____

_____

_____

_____

_____

_____

_____

_____

_____

_____

_____

_____

_____

_____

_____

_____

_____

_____

_____

_____

_____

_____

Day 16
The Catch

"God is with her she will not fall..." (Psalm 46:5) NIV

It's amazing how we allow other people and things to discourage us from following our dreams and goals. You know that time, when you had your mind made up to take that leap of faith, and just do it. You shared with those close to you your next move; instead of receiving encouragement, you're faced with dream killers and naysayers. Next you have taken on the mindset of those who doubted you, causing you to give up, and never revisit the idea again.

Many of us are stuck because of fear! Fear has a way of holding your mind and actions hostage. It creeps into our minds under the disguise of doubt and once it settles it changes into its true character, which is fear. As a result, our plans and actions become idle and if we're not careful they will die.

And what exactly are we afraid of? Is it the unknown? Maybe it's the predicted doors that will shut our efforts to pursue the dream? Perhaps we are simply afraid of failing!

I can remember when our boys were babies, and they were learning how to walk. Falling was a simply part of the process. In the beginning, they would fall more than they took steps. Yet, in their little toddler mind, they were already programming themselves to persevere. Eventually, the hard work paid off, and our house was never the same, LOL.

Application

What if we could go back to that childlike determination, where nothing took our focus off the goal? Where we were not afraid of the setbacks or the downfalls? What if we took to heart Isaiah 41:10 (NKJV) which says, "Fear not, for I am with you; be not dismayed, for I am your God. I will strengthen you, yes I will help you, I will uphold you with My righteous right hand."

When you know whose you are and the power that comes along with that connection, nothing and no one can stop you. Even if you stumble along the way, you will not fall for you are in His hand! By seeking God, we are able to identify our purpose in life. Living out that purpose is not always easy. Although the road is set by God, the walk is not always simple. Sometimes we may find ourselves on shaky ground, and other times we may fall. However for the child of God, falling down doesn't mean failing. For when we fall, the righteous hand of God is right there to catch us!

I will pursue my dreams by doing...

_____

_____

_____

_____

_____

_____

_____

_____

_____

_____

_____

Day 17
Tailor Made

" *I* will praise You, for I am fearfully and wonderfully made…" (Psalm 139:14) NKJV

There is so much work that goes into being a woman. Don't get me wrong, I absolutely love being a woman. I describe myself as being a girly girl, but there are times that the upkeep is a bit much. I mean, we have to make hair and nail appointments, work out, make sure our bras and panties match, wear the right undergarments to keep everything smooth and intact, and the list goes on and on and on!

If we were to be honest, sometimes that stuff can consume us completely. We all have that one girlfriend who is into herself a bit too much. You know the one that everything is perfect and in place, taking 3 hours to accomplish that perfect goal…yes her! True enough, we should have pride in how we look and present ourselves; unfortunately we sometimes put more effort into our outer appearance verses enhancing the substance within.

Our attitude, character, and spirit should be the most attractive feature that we possess. The moment we realize that according to Genesis 1:26 we were created in the very image of God, which gives us all the confidence. The time, effort, and purpose that God has, is tailor made for His perfect will concerning our lives.

Application

When we get dressed, we like our clothes to fit. Oh, we all have experienced seeing an outfit online or in the store that looks amazing on the hanger, but when we try it on, it's a completely different look. It becomes evident that this garment is not for me. Yet, when it comes to the Word of God, there is a tailor made word for you.

No matter where you find yourself in life, there is a word that is fitting and perfect for every situation. When you realize that the best accessory any of us can obtain is the Spirit of God, your dress to impress days will turn into dress for success days. For it is by the aid of the Holy Spirit that our light can cast away any darkness. What lady doesn't like a little bling!

As you move throughout this day, no matter what comes your way, know that you are created to handle it. For you have been tailor made by the hands of a perfect God who has left you with a tailored made word for a time such as this!

1: God has created me to…?

_____

_____

_____

2: I will let my light shine by….?

_____

_____

_____

3: My Tailor Made scripture for my situation is….?

_____

_____

_____

Tailor Made

Day 18

My Sister's Keeper

"Let each of you look out not only for his own interests, but also for the interest of others" (Philippians 2:4) NKJV

There's nothing better after a long stressful week than getting together with some girlfriends, over good food paired with memorable conversation. Every woman has an inner circle, a crew, a selected group of ladies she can count on. This circle is not just a sisterhood, no this circle is a secret society and all they ask for is trust! Stories and secrets are shared in this circle that will go to the grave. Not everyone can know everything about you, but in this circle, you are safe to be you. It's the no judgment zone!

Yet even in our closest knit circles, responsibility and obligations are still warranted. We are responsible and obligated to contribute to the success of those close to us. That means holding them accountable, being that extra push to aid them in their destiny. But most importantly, it means to pray for them. See a real sister circle is one where vulnerability lives; a place where you can share your weakness and where your dreams have no limits because of the constant support.

God has a way of connecting us with people who are purposely placed in our lives. He blesses us with dreams and goals to succeed. He also surrounds us with individuals that keep us on track to fulfill the intended purpose.

My question today is, what do you contribute to your circle? Are you the sister that prays for those included in your circle? Do you share their passion for their dreams? Are you pushing them and holding them accountable to reach their goals?

Application

If you can't answer yes to these questions, now is the time to start. We must realize that God is an intentional God. Everything He does has a purpose. So it's not by accident that you are surrounded by your sister circle, or that you click with certain individuals as if you've known them for a life time. It's all God's design! However, we are obligated to contribute to the success of the sisterhood. The same way your sister girlfriend is in your life for a reason, so are you in theirs.

Not only are we placed in various circles to be poured into with encouragement and wisdom, we must also pour out support and accountability to challenge one another. Proverbs 27:17 (NIV) says, "As iron sharpens iron, so one person sharpens another." Your blessing could be connected to your sister's success. Keep her focus, keep her prayed up, and keep her motivated to see her dreams come true. God will bless you in the process!

I'm holding my Sister Circle accountable by...

_____
_____
_____
_____
_____
_____
_____
_____
_____
_____

Her Walk Day 18

Day 19
Ouch...That Hurts

" *It* was good for me that I have been afflicted, that I may l earn your statutes" (Psalm 119:71) NKJV

Isn't it interesting how things like hurt, pain, sadness, and heartache grasp our attention? We don't consider the signs leading up to the hurt. For example, when the voice within says that's the wrong move, yet you proceed.

God speaks to us in so many different ways. Sometimes His voice is obvious and loud as thunder, while other times it's a mere faint whisper. If we're honest, there are times we ignore His voice, confuse it with our own voice, all while trying to rationalize and make sense of it all. Then there are times when we are forced to acknowledge, hear, and take heed of His instructions. Sometimes that "force" comes by way of affliction.

I can remember being a child watching my mother iron our clothes for school. I was so fascinated by the design of the iron. The fact that it had these little holes on the bottom and this "chimney" (at least that's what I called it...lol) on top that would produce this smoke, was just intriguing to me. My mother seeing my big brown eyes light up every time she would iron, gave me the disclosure, "this is NOT a toy, and you can hurt yourself if you touch it."

Application

One day she was ironing clothes and turned around to grab the next piece of clothing to iron. This was my chance, if I move fast enough I can get a quick reach in and finally make contact. Welp, needless to say, contact was made, and it came in the form of blisters on my fingertips, in addition to the punishment I received from my mother. Rightfully so! The lesson I learned from this disobedient act, has carried over into my adulthood; listen, even when you don't understand why!

Every situation and experience we encounter is an opportunity to learn and grow; even through hurt and pain. While it's not comfortable or easy to deal with, the design and purpose is to shape and mold you into something greater and stronger. Isaiah 55:8 (NKJV) says, "For My thoughts are not your thoughts, nor are your ways, My ways, says the Lord." Yet in times of hurt, pain, sickness, or distress, we must not allow these emotions to block the purpose and the lesson that God has intended for us to receive.

Reflect

_____

_____

_____

_____

_____

_____

_____

_____

_____

_____

_____

_____

Ouch...That's Hurts

_____
_____
_____
_____
_____
_____
_____
_____
_____
_____
_____
_____
_____
_____
_____
_____
_____
_____
_____
_____
_____
_____
_____
_____
_____
_____
_____
_____

Day 20
Find HER...Keep HER

" *And* that you put on the new man which was created according to God, in true righteousness and holiness" (Ephesians 4:24) NKJV

There's something about being a woman. We are complex at times but yet simple. We love hard, yet always willing to love freely. We're strong but soft.We're sweet but bitter at times. We are producers by nature.

- Give us an egg...we'll give you life
- Give us a pen...we'll write a book
- Give us a house...we'll make it a home
- Give us a man...we'll show you a King
- Give us a little...we'll give you a lot

We know how to turn nothing into something. It's in our anatomy, and it's who we are! We're able to see beyond the potential of something and connect with its purpose. Proverbs 19:21 (NIV) says, "Many are the plans in a person's heart, but it is the Lord's purpose that prevails." There's a difference between potential and purpose. Potential says this is what could be, but purpose declares this is what it WILL BE! As women, we're able to do just that. We're able to see the purpose in everyone's life and help them reach their full potential. Except ours!

It's so easy to get lost in everyone's world. As wives we become helpmeets to our husbands, and suitable to all their needs. As a parent, we become mothers to our children teaching them their ABC's, their manors, and the Do's and Don'ts of life. As a friend we become the listening ear, the shoulder to cry on, the person to rely on...just to name a few. And in the midst of it all, we find ourselves lost, searching for an identity to call our own.

Transparent Moment; I can remember being in that space where I became so consumed with trying to be the best wife and mother, making our children such a priority in my life that I forgot what I liked. I lost touch of my goals and dreams, I was losing me! My husband and I had a conversation in which he asked, what personal goals I wanted to accomplish in the next 3 years. The fact that I could not provide an answer was my personal wake up call, realizing I needed to find me!

God has created us for a purpose! He has placed gifts inside us to compliment our purpose, yet we get so distracted with other people and things, that we lose sight of our own purpose. It's easy to get lost, but thank God we can find our identity and purpose in Christ!

Application

Seeking God and praying for my purpose to be revealed to me began to establish some balance in my life, which I must say has always been on my bucket list...FIND BALANCE!!! Before, I thought I never had the time to really pursue my goals and dreams. I would always make the excuse of saying, "but the boys." One day in prayer God spoke to me and said, "I did not bless you with your children to hold you back, I blessed you with them to push you forward!"

That was the day I found her! I found me! My viewpoint on life, being a wife, and mother changed. I was no longer just alive, from that moment on I began to live!

Find the YOU that has been missing. The YOU that

you've been placing on hold. The YOU that God has called you to become. The YOU, which is waiting to be birthed! Find her, she's worth being discovered! And once you find her, make sure you keep her!

Goals I want to accomplish...

_____

_____

_____

_____

_____

_____

_____

_____

_____

_____

_____

_____

_____

_____

_____

_____

_____

_____

_____

_____

_____

Day 21
The Power of N.O.

"*B*ut as for you, you meant evil against me; but God meant it for good…" (Genesis 50:20) NKJV

It's the word that everyone hates. It's short and straight to the point. From an infant to adulthood, we never want to hear the word NO! There's something about those two letters, when placed in this order, the sound of it automatically speaks a negative tone. I mean think about it, there is no nice way to say NO! You can try to put other words around it as a buffer, but it's pointless because no means NO!

What if we could turn that negative word into a positive one? What if we could view those letters from a different lens that would shed some positive light? What if I told you, the next time someone tells you NO, walk away hearing the words, New Opportunity (N.O.).

We allow the word NO to stop us in our tracks, never to move forward. We allow the word NO to be the end all be all; but who says we have to accept NO for an answer? Yes, technically it's an answer, but is it the answer for our plans, goals, and dreams? Granted, nothing comes easy and rejection is part of the growth process but when pursuing your dreams, doors will get closed in your face. You will hear the word NO more often than you hear the word yes. Just know that when this happens, a new opportunity is waiting for you!

Application

We must not give up in our pursuit of happiness and becoming whole. I believe the word NO was created to weed out the strong from the weak. Not everyone can bounce back from a NO. It has the power to be devastating and painful. But I've come to learn that only you can give power to words. You determine what you will allow to shake you verses move you.

Sometimes, God will take us on a detour. We have it all made up in our mind how it's going to happen, when it's going to happen, and where it's going to happen... and then there's God's plan. The roadblocks that come in the form of a NO are purposely placed to take us off our planned road and place us in the Will of God.

Isaiah 54:17(NKJV) tells us that "No weapon formed against you shall prosper..." This means being told NO you can't do something, or NO you're not good enough, can not take root in a child of God! You are a conqueror, a fighter, and you are a believer! View someone telling you NO as a time to adjust, evaluate, and reset. Turn your lemons into lemonade. Take that N.O. and turn it into a New Opportunity! A new way of thinking, a new route, a new plan. You have what it takes to succeed.

I was told No regarding...

_____

_____

_____

_____

But my New Opportunity will be...

_____

_____

_____

Her Walk Day 21

Day 22
Me, Myself, and I

" *For* no one ever hated his own flesh, but nourishes and cherishes it, just as the Lord does the church" (Ephesians 5:29) NKJV

When was the last time you had a "me" day? You know, a day when you put everyone's issues on the shelf, and put you first. A day when you pamper yourself with doing the things you love. Such as going to the library to read your favorite book, treating yourself to a mani/pedi, or doing some retail therapy. When was the last time you took yourself on a date?

Self-love is vital in our Christian development. Of all the things God created, He made you and me in His image, and for that reason, we should take pride in self. I've come to learn that in order for me to be a great wife, mom, daughter, and friend, I must take care of self-first! There are moments when I feel guilty for taking time out for myself. As a result, the needs of those closest to me became more important to pursue. But I found the more I ignored myself, the further my name dropped on my to-do list.

Being a child of God comes with a certain level of "God-fidence."

1 Corinthians 3:16 (NKJV) says, "Do you not know that you are the temple of God and that the Spirit of God dwells in you?" As a vessel that carries the Holy Spirit, this affords you a sense of pride. Knowing who you are and whose you are is key, in every Christian's development. Granted we all have room for growth, but when you love yourself, you don't mind going through the growing pains that life brings because you recognize that it's for your good.

Application

The well-being of your mind, body, and soul must be on your priority list. Having the ability to think with a clear conscience allows you to hear God with an open ear. Having a body that is healthy allows you to serve God at a level of excellence, and having a spirit that is full allows you to worship Him in spirit and in truth.

The next time you have an opportunity to have some Me, Myself, and I time, indulge in it. Use that time to regroup your thoughts, to relax your body, and to reconnect your spirit. In this life we are given one body; take care of it and love the skin you're in. Today do something for you! Treat yourself to a spa day or go and purchase your favorite perfume, you deserve it!

My next Me, Myself, and I day will be on_____

_____ I

have the following planned_____

_____

_____

_____

_____

_____

_____

_____

_____

_____

Her Walk Day 22

Day 23
Jackpot!

"*May He grant you according to your heart's desire, and fulfill your purpose*" (Psalm 20:4) NKJV

Have you ever wanted something in life but it seemed so impossible to obtain? Some might call it wishful thinking, but in your eyes, it's your dreams, goals, or purpose. It's the thing that keeps you up at night, urging you to go for it.

What if I told you that your dreams aren't as unattainable as they seem? That you can actually accomplish your goal, that you can fulfill your purpose in life. Yes, it can happen!

See God doesn't just want us to live and simply exist because He created us. He wants us to have life and life MORE abundantly (John 10:10). He wants us to live out our dreams, for He is the one that gave them to us. It was God that planted the idea in your mind to create that product, to open your own business, or to go after your dream job. The thought came from Him, now it's up to you to make it a reality. You can do it!

Everything that you need to succeed, you already have. Each of us was created with gifts and talents specific to our purpose to ensure we reach our full potential. That thing that you're naturally good at, that comes second nature to you; is the very thing that makes you unique. It's your niche; it's your own personal Jackpot!

Application

My only question is, what's holding you back? Is it fear, doubt, or perhaps insecurities? All of these are weapons of the enemy. But our weapon (the Bible) tells us that "No weapon formed against you, shall prosper" (Isaiah 54:17) NKJV. Maybe what's holding you back is outside forces such as other people or not gaining the support for your vision. Well, guess what, they're not supposed to! It's YOUR vision.

Your jackpot is full of treasures waiting to be released. Whatever your heart desires, know you're the only one that can make them a reality. Life is too short to live it unfulfilled. Your dreams are the road map to your purpose. Let God order your steps and lead you to a life worth living.

I can apply this devotional to my life by...

_____

_____

_____

_____

_____

_____

_____

_____

_____

_____

_____

_____

_____

_____

_____

Jackpot!

_____
_____
_____
_____
_____
_____
_____
_____
_____
_____
_____
_____
_____
_____
_____
_____
_____
_____
_____
_____
_____
_____
_____
_____
_____
_____
_____
_____
_____

Her Walk Day 23

Day 24

Nope...NOT TODAY!

"These things have I spoken unto you, that my joy might remain in you, and that your joy might be full" (John 15:11) NKJV

Every day is a day of challenge and opportunity to learn. I found that when I start my day off with prayer, asking God to set my path and to keep me on track, I'm off to a successful start. Even when your day begins on a positive note, it can still end with frustration.

One thing that this life has taught me is that you control how you respond to people and situations. How many times do we allow circumstances, people, and things to have control over our actions and reactions? The enemy is always looking for ways to get us off track mentally and spiritually. We must not allow his evil tactics and conniving ways to bring our character into question in the sight of others and especially not in the sight of God!

When we are faced with adversity, distress, or just plain old mess, we usually give our 2 cents and flare up, granting the enemy full access to the core of our soul which is our JOY!

Application

Your joy has a way of keeping you centered when walls are closing in on you. Joy keeps you from lashing out at that coworker who's always trying to push your buttons. Joy gives you balance when life is trying to keep you on shaky ground. It's that place mentally and spiritually that you can go to within, that is sure to renew, restore, and remind you of the promises of God! It's having that insight to the Word of God and allowing yourself, your feelings, and your attitude to become consumed and overtaken. It's when the Word of God becomes the "LIVING WORD" within you. You're able to depend on it, and every time you're able to tap into that core it brings about a peace that surpasses all understanding. It's your JOY! And it must be protected by ANY means necessary!

The risk is too costly for your joy to go unprotected. You begin to operate out of character, you risk putting relationships on thin ice, as well as regretting something that you said. Bottom line, it's simply not worth it! Daily we must make up in our mind that no matter what comes our way, our joy will NOT be tampered with. Nope, not today!

Today I'm going to protect my joy by...

_____
_____
_____
_____
_____
_____
_____
_____
_____
_____
_____
_____
_____

Nope...NOT TODAY!

Her Walk Day 24

Day 25

W.I.N.

" *To* everything there is a season, a time for every purpose under heaven" (Ecclesiastes 3:1) NKJV

It waits for no one, there's never enough of it, and it's the one constant that remains, you guessed right; I'm talking about time. I find it interesting how much of a major role timing plays in determining success or failure. Think about it, you can have a plan completely sketched out with every detail in mind. All your ducks are in a row, ready to launch, and the only thing that can prevent it from moving forward is the right timing.

There are times when you are in a season of NOW! It's time to make a move. God has already given you a green light, your prayers have been answered, it's time to execute, and put your faith to work. In your season of NOW, it's time to W.I.N!! Time to Work It Now (W.I.N)!

One thing about seasons is that they come and they go. If you have prayed about a situation and have received your confirmation, then it's time to W.I.N. Your season of NOW is depending on you to make it happen. This is the time you put your plan into action. When you step out on faith and jump into your destiny, it's time for your purpose to be birthed for everyone to see and benefit from it. No longer will you allow fear and doubt to have a stronghold on your plans, goals, and aspirations. This is your season to W.I.N!

Application

We often allow our season of now to run pass us, because we're not ready or ill prepared. We didn't plan our work or work our plan to make proper preparations to secure our success. Don't let this be your story. If you are still waiting to receive your green light, your "yes," or confirmation from God, know that you can still WIN by preparing for your season of change.

Now is the time to become a believer of your own dreams. Work IT Now! Plan, strategize and research. Do the work securing your success to win.

I will to do the following so I can W.I.N...

_____
_____
_____
_____
_____
_____
_____
_____
_____
_____
_____
_____
_____
_____
_____
_____
_____
_____
_____

Her Walk Day 25

Day 26

It's All Good

"And we know that all things work together for good to those who love God, to those who are called according to His purpose" (Romans 8:28) NKJV

Have you ever been caught in a storm? Not the kind of storm that brings rain and floods. But the kind of storm that life brings? You know the one where the bills are pouring down, your job seems to get foggy each day, your friends seem to be wishy washy, and your personal relationship appears to be sinking by the minute, yeah, that kind of storm?

You know how it is; one thing just leads to another. Instead of seeing the light at the end of the tunnel, the days go on, and the tunnel becomes more narrow. Have you been there? Maybe you're reading this saying, "I'm there NOW!"

We can rest assure that in this life, all things are temporary! While it's easy to state this fact, the harsh reality is that there are times when we are in a storm and it seems like an eternity. Yet it is the Word of God that constantly reminds us of the benefits that come along with being a Child of God.

While it may seem overwhelming and agonizing, we are reminded by the Word of God, it's ALL Good! For those of us who are called according to His purpose, the glass for US is always half full! We serve a God that can turn a messy situation into a MESSAGE, one who can turn a test into a TESTIMONY.

Application

Life is not meant to be experienced without its transgressions, it's meant to be experienced through trial and tribulations, but ultimately growth. Our growing pains are diminished when we trust God's Word for our individual situations. To know without a shadow of a doubt that whatever trial or test we may face, it will work for our good. As beneficiaries of this promise, faithfulness and obedience must be present in our lives.

When we are faced with stormy days, our faithfulness to our daily reading and meditation begins to slip away, which causes us to lose sight of His promises for our lives. As a result, we run for shelter taking matters into our own hands instead of dealing with them on our knees!

We must remember that we serve a God who is very present in our lives. No matter what storms may come our way, it is the hand of God that covers us and keeps us as the storms pass by. For this reason alone, we can look our test and trials in the face and declare…It's ALL Good!

Reflect

_____

_____

_____

_____

_____

_____

_____

_____

_____

_____

It's All Good

Her Walk Day 26

Day 27

Talk to the Hand

"*Your* hand shall be lifted against your adversaries, and all your enemies shall be cut off" (Micah 5:9) NKJV

There are times in life when you simply have to throw your hands up and move on. Sometimes it's that family member that is in need of something; that girlfriend that calls with her drama filled life, or a misunderstanding in a relationship. At some point, we all run out of answers, money to give, and an ear to lend. Every person has their breaking point.

However, those moments and situations listed above are usually manageable. What happens when you find yourself with your back in the corner and nowhere to run or escape? What happens when you run out of words to say? When your thoughts have become discombobulated from over thinking a situation? Where do you go? Who do you run to?

Life has its own way of putting us in uncomfortable situations in which God has created to test us. How long we stay in the situation can be based upon if we've learned the lesson or passed the test. Yet and still, we must be able to find that strength within to praise God even in an uncomfortable situation.

The people and vices that come in our paths, are there to push us toward something greater. We view them as pulling us down instead of pushing us forward. Even in the midst of a storm, you have a reason to praise God! In nature, rain is needed for growth to take place. Such as life! You will never truly know your strength until you've experienced being knocked down. For it is at that time that the mental decision has to be made. How long will I allow myself to stay in this position?

During those times in my life where I found myself asking the same question, it was my faith in God and the praise in my heart that gave me the strength to pull myself up. When life has knocked you down, the first thing that should go up is your hands! Surrender your weakness to God, and your praise to Him. There is a strength to be found in weakness. 2 Corinthians 12:9 (NKJV) says, "And He said to me, 'My grace is sufficient for you, for My strength is made perfect in weakness'."

Application

How do you praise your way back on your feet? How do you lift your hands up against your adversaries? First, you have to surrender and then you must submit! We feel like we have what it takes to get through a situation. We think we know ourselves better than anyone else. We find ourselves trying to stand up against those things that are in our way to harm us, while God is waiting for us to kneel down and surrender to Him.

Throwing your hands up is a tactic of confusion to the enemy. The enemy thinks you are giving up, but the all seeing eye of God views it as a sign of you surrendering it all to Him and submitting to His will in your life!

The next time you find yourself in a situation where your back is in the corner, and life has knocked you down to your knees, lift your hands up and watch God step in and take over.

Reflect

_____

_____

_____

Her Walk Day 27

Day 28

Don't Worry. Be Happy!

" *T*herefore do not worry about tomorrow, for tomorrow will worry about its own things…" (Matthew 6:34) NKJV

Waking up in the morning, you never know what kind of day you will have. Some days are a mystery and others come with preconceived issues. Be it health challenges, job security, loss of friendships, financial contention, or family drama; no one wakes up anticipating a bad day.

The good news is you are in control of you! How you respond to today's events and the outcome, is solely based on your perception. Despite the reality of your circumstances, how you perceive and respond is all that matters. You can choose to worry, or you can choose to be happy. Either way, your circumstance doesn't change but how you deal with it, does.

Every day we wake up is a gift from God. It's a fresh new start, a clean slate, a new opportunity to tackle the demands that come along. It's important for us to capture and live in the moment. Within a few hours, (24 to be exact) this day is gone, never to return again. The only thing that will remain constant is Jesus Christ. Hebrews 13:8 (NKJV) says, "Jesus Christ is the same yesterday, today, and forever." Today is responsible for its own unique challenges; some new, some old. The fact remains that tomorrow will present a whole new set of challenges.

Application

How do you embrace a gift that is also equipped with a few setbacks? You may decide to cross that bridge when you get to it, while others may say push it off until tomorrow. I've tried both and neither gave me the outcome I was looking for. The only technique that has been successful is to pray your way through!

That's right, pray! If it sounds simple, that's because it is. There's only one person who knows what stumbling blocks are headed your way. There's only one person that knows what today, tomorrow, and the next day will bring. So why not seek Him first! Psalm 16:8 (NKJV) says, "I have set the Lord always before me; because He is at my right hand I shall not be moved."

Don't allow yesterday, today, or tomorrow's events to move you into a space of worry. Be happy that we serve an all seeing, all knowing God, who is able to keep us in good and bad times.

Reflect

_____

_____

_____

_____

_____

_____

_____

_____

_____

_____

_____

_____

_____

Don't Worry. Be Happy!

　　　　　Her Walk Day 28

Day 29

Don't Forget your C.R.O.W.N.

" *Y*ou shall also be a crown of glory in the hand of the Lord" (Isaiah 62:3) NKJV

As a little girl, I remember the excitement that came along with receiving my gold crown at Burger King. It was something about the crown that made my day. Feeling like a true princess while demolishing a Junior Whopper, that crown was what I lived for. I would wear that cardboard crown everywhere! It was the best accessory any burger could have and I was sure to wear it as long as it last.

As you get older your appetite changes and so does your perspective on life. Conversely, there are times when something from your childhood teaches you a lesson as an adult. At that time, my Burger King crown and I were inseparable.

Let's fast forward to being a young adult. While seeking God and having a desire to draw closer to Him, I came across 1 Peter 2:9, "But you are a chosen generation, a royal priesthood, a holy nation, His own special people, that you may proclaim the praises of Him who called you out of darkness into His marvelous light;" Reading this scripture reminded me of feeling like royalty as a child from my Burger King crown days; but this gave me confirmation that being royalty was actually a reality in the sight of God.

Application

Now as an adult, I make sure I don't leave home without my C.R.O.W.N.

C-Christ: As you go forth in this day be sure to carry Christ with you in your heart and mind. As a constant reminder that you are a Child of God that comes with direction and protection. Allow Him to do both as you go about your day.

R- Righteousness: Your personal experiences in Christ enhances your faith walk. It sustains your truth in Him beyond your experience. Whatever direction life takes on this journey, stand firm on knowing that we serve a God of righteousness who will equip us with all that we need to endure.

O-Obedience: Typically, we are motivated to please man. Be it our boss, our teachers, our mates, etc. Yet we must remember where our true loyalty lies. Obedience to God's Word and Will positions us in direct alignment with receiving His blessings.

W-Worth: Knowing that you are chosen by God and predestined for royalty is a foundation to stand firm on. There is always something or someone attempting to challenge our capabilities. Nevertheless, when you know your worth in God that confidence will strengthen you to carry on.

N- Nobility: Having a crown of glory upon your head will cause you to keep your head held high! Despite what people do or say, despite the roadblocks that may come your way; you are already equipped and capable of accomplishing your goal. Remember you are a child of the King!

Before you walk out that door today, entering into the world, remember one thing, the C.R.O.W.N must lead first!

Don't Forget your C.R.O.W.N.

Reflect

_____

_____

_____

_____

_____

_____

_____

_____

_____

_____

_____

_____

_____

_____

_____

_____

_____

_____

_____

_____

_____

_____

_____

_____

_____

_____

_____

_____

Day 30
White Flag

"Casting all your care upon Him, He cares for you" (1Peter 5:7) NKJV

Ever felt like turning in your adult card for the day? A day where you are free from, laundry, work, cooking, cleaning, etc. A day where you can relax, eat a bowl of ice cream, and watch your favorite movie. Most definitely one of those days!

As much as we do for others, we absolutely deserve one of those days! The reality is, we have to schedule that type of day, and even then, circumstances will interrupt our "Me" time. We all can attest to those days and moments in life where we just want to yell, "I give up, or "I quit," even waving the white flag, of surrender.

Transparent moment; there are times where I want to be that superwoman who knows what she's cooking for dinner a week prior, whose home looks like it belongs in a magazine, who works out 4-6 times a week! But the truth of the matter is I'm not Superwoman. I don't have super powers, and I don't wear a cape. However, when I'm feeling overwhelmed and drained, I go and grab my imaginary "S" shirt and SURRENDER.

Application

God did not create us to have all the answers for life's shortcomings; if we did there would be no need for Jesus. We try to stand up against life's curve balls, instead of making the decision to kneel. We subject ourselves to unnecessary stress due to the exhaustion that comes along with carrying the load. All the while, Christ is saying "Come to me, all you who labor and are heavy laden, and I will give you rest." (Matthew 11:28) NKJV

The love that Christ has for us is second to none. He

doesn't take pride and joy in seeing us overwhelmed and stressed. The source of our strength is in Him and Him alone. We ourselves might not have super powers, but we serve a God that is able to speak things into existence, provide health with one touch, make the blind see, and the lame walk. Whatever it is that you're faced with today, whatever it is that you're carrying today, wave your white flag and surrender it all to Him. For He is more than capable of handling it all!

Today I'm going to surrender these things to God

_____

_____

_____

_____

_____

_____

_____

_____

_____

_____

_____

_____

_____

_____

White Flag

124   Her Walk Day 30

One Way

"**J**esus said to him, I am the way, the truth, and the life. No one comes to the Father except through Me" (John 14:6) NKJV

I can recall first receiving my driver's license, I was so excited! Good-bye to the embarrassment of my mother dropping me off at the mall and my brother chauffeuring me around. Ahhh yes, my first taste of independence.

That excitement rapidly left as soon as I began to rack up those tickets. Failure to make a complete stop, speeding 15 miles over the limit, I even received a ticket for driving down a one-way street. Has that ever happened to you? It was a complete accident. There were no parked cars on the street to remind me that I was going the wrong way. It was late at night, so there weren't any other cars traveling up or down this particular street. Oh, and I didn't see the "One Way" signs on the road. Needless to say I'm thankful I got that ticket, because matters could have turned out worse.

I can attest to that statement in both the spirit and the flesh! I'm sure we all can. All of us have experienced those moments when the hand of God stopped us dead in our tracks, preventing matters from getting worse. We all can relate to living life, and at some point not being able to see the signs of caution to turn us around into the right direction.

Application

But thanks be to God for His Son Jesus! Even when we detour off our journey trying to do things our way, He is there to place us back on track. All of our routes may differ; some with roadblocks, detours, and even construction. We are all striving to arrive at the same final destination!

One Way

Many of us are guilty of carpooling; focused on helping others find their place, which comes at a risk of losing our own direction. The road less traveled is not too hard to find for it only travels one way, leading to an eternal life in Heaven.

If you feel like you're lost, can't find your way, and missed the signs which steered you off track. There is a Man waiting to show you the way! His directions will never mislead you. His instructions will always guide you. Try Jesus Christ, He is the way!

This now completes your journey, take your walk with Christ!

**Psalm 32:8 NKJV "I will instruct you and teach you in the way you should go, I will guide you with my eye" Reflect

_____
_____
_____
_____

Romans 10:9 NIV "If you declare with your mouth, "Jesus is Lord", and believe in your heart that God raised him from the dead, you will be saved."

Reflect

_____
_____
_____
_____

John 3:16 KJV "For God so loved the world that he gave his only begotten son that who so ever believe in him, should not parish but have everlasting life."

Reflect

_____

_____

_____

_____

_____

_____

_____

_____

_____

_____

_____

_____

_____

_____

_____

_____

_____

_____

_____

One Way